ARTPRIZE

Laura Isaac, *10000 Hours La Grande Vitesse*, 2012; photo: Rick Treur.

How a Radically
Open Competition
Transformed a City
and Changed the Way
We Think about Art

From left to right: Michael Peoples, *Will You Still Need Me, Will You Still Feed Me*, 2013; The Arts Screwed Collective, 2011; Heechan Kim, *Form #8*, 2010; Tracy Van Duinen, Todd Osborne, Phil Schuster, *Metaphorest*, 2011; Rob Bliss, *The Hundred Thousand Paper Planes & Melodies Over Monroe Project*, 2009.

It's time to reboot the conversation between artists and the public. ArtPrize will be a celebration of art, design, and innovation that will bring artists and the public together like never before.

— ARTPRIZE FOUNDER RICK DEVOS, APRIL 23, 2009

INTRODUCTION

Rick DeVos
ArtPrize Founder

The future is a funny thing. We can dream, we can make plans, but ultimately events unfold and we need to figure out ways to adapt. I find myself thinking about this when looking back at the history of ArtPrize. What originally started out as a "what if," a raw idea, a sketch of an experiment, has flourished and grown into an event (and dare I say phenomenon) embraced and owned by an entire community.

I will admit that I didn't think through the full implications of successfully implementing the thing we wanted to try in 2009. The "what ifs" of the idea itself (large prize, decentralized process, massive public engagement, among others) were compelling enough. I suppose in some way that is the spirit I wanted, and still want, ArtPrize to inspire in participants every year. For artists to think *What if I try something new?* Or, *What if I put my work in a place that seems, frankly, weird and people see and respond to it who I wouldn't have thought would ever see it otherwise?* And for venues to think *What if we thought of our physical space like a gallery, at least for a few weeks?* And myriad other questions. The thing that you realize after a while is that there is always work, nothing is ever "figured out," there will forever be surprises. There are always things to change, always things to improve, and most importantly, always things to learn.

After five events, that original, raw idea has birthed a vibrant, vital institution that is now woven into the identity, texture, and excitement of the community it lives in and partners with. I find myself, having relatively recently become a parent, reflecting on this growing idea of ArtPrize in an oddly parental way. Obviously proud of the growth, of the maturity, of the changes, of the possibilities. Concerned about what interventions to make, how to shape its maturity, what boundaries to draw. I am learning a lot in these parallel processes, but in both I'm filled with an overwhelming sense of gratitude. Grateful for a team and partners that share the vision and are excited about continuing forward. Grateful for a broader community that so wholeheartedly embraces and supports the project. Grateful to be blessed with the challenge of stewarding, caring for, and guiding young life.

ArtPrize is an organic construct. It will continue to evolve, change, and grow. Thanks for being a part of that process. The best is yet to come.

This page: Jan Dean, *Transformation,* 2013. Opposite: Ryan C. Doyle, Teddy Lo, Joshua "Bacon" McAninch, *Gon KiRin,* 2013.

Lynda Cole, *Rain*, 2011

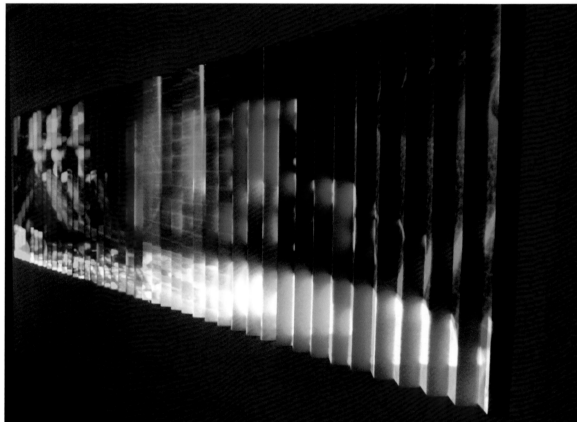

You'd have to have come to Grand Rapids, Michigan, to actually see what it's done. The point is you have hundreds and hundreds of artists who have given up their lives for a period of time, who have spent huge amounts of money going to incredible energy, expense, and time to create these projects. I think very few of them really believe that they actually have a chance at really winning much of anything, just based on numbers. It's like a lottery. But they're here giving their hearts to it. . . . Everywhere you look there are objects, and projections, and performances . . . And the scale, I have to say I'm really quite astonished. There is just so much.

—ADAM WEINBERG, ALICE PRATT BROWN DIRECTOR, WHITNEY MUSEUM OF AMERICAN ART,
     2009 ARTPRIZE GUEST LECTURER

From left to right: Andreas von Gehr, *Rebiogehr*, 2012; Complex Movements, *Three Phases*, 2012; Jimmy Kuehnle, *You Wear What I Wear*, 2009; photo: Vince Dudzinski.

Adonna Khare, *Elephants* (detail), 2012

THE ARTPRIZE PHENOMENON

Dustin Dwyer

We watched the announcement on a cool April day in 2009. The chairs lined up in the morning sun, the slim podium, the limestone pillars of the old Civic Auditorium rising in the background.

The first person to speak was Jim Dunlap, a banker and leader in the effort to bring life to downtown Grand Rapids. His hair: neatly parted. His suit: dark.

"I want to begin by saying the announcement you're about to hear will have tremendous impact on our region," Dunlap said. "Something the rest of the [country] and the world will be aware of and talking about even before we're finished here this morning."

We didn't completely believe him.

Dunlap introduced Rick DeVos, a 27-year-old with a famous last name, at least in this town. His hair: meticulously unkempt. His suit: not a suit.

"I've been thinking for several years that Grand Rapids needed a really great signature international festival or event of some type," DeVos said. "Something that would celebrate creativity and innovation and beauty, and that tapped into the great tradition of public art and design in West Michigan."

DeVos said what he had in mind was a competition.

A great big banner unfurled behind him.

"ARTPRIZE," it said. "PUBLIC VOTE."

"That was fun," DeVos said.

———

Anyone could compete in ArtPrize. Any space downtown could be a venue to show work: business lobbies, sidewalks, parking lots, parks. The prize money was huge: $250,000 for first place, $449,000 total. All of it would be decided by popular vote.

We understood the rules. That didn't necessarily mean we understood what ArtPrize would *be*.

Was it an economic development tool? A cultural conversation starter? Or a radical new way to judge art? Would it bring life to a fledgling downtown? Would it lead us out of the rust belt and into the creative class economy? Or would it lob a $449,000 hand-grenade at the cloistered, coastal, big-city arts establishment?

Yes.

Just five months after ArtPrize was announced, the first competition began. A total of 1,262 artists signed up to participate. Their work would show in 159 different venues within a three square mile area.

Rob Bliss, *The Hundred Thousand Paper Planes & Melodies Over Monroe Project*, 2009

Art was everywhere downtown. We couldn't see all of it if we tried, but we tried.

A study by Grand Valley State University economics students would later estimate that 200,000 people visited downtown during the first ArtPrize, creating as much as $7 million in new economic activity. It would have been more than that if businesses had been prepared.

On one Sunday afternoon, an estimated 20,000 people filled Monroe Avenue to watch a 20-year-old college student and his friends dump tens of thousands of paper airplanes off the tops of buildings. Afterward, the crush of customers was too much for many restaurants to handle. Some ran out of food. Others were closed to begin with. Sunday is traditionally a slow day for downtown Grand Rapids businesses. ArtPrize proved it didn't have to be.

Yes, ArtPrize was an economic development tool. A powerful one.

But it wasn't just that. We talked about the art constantly. In coffee shops and cubicles, at restaurants and bus stops, in person and online, we talked about art. We talked about what we loved, what we hated. We argued.

ArtPrize had changed the conversation, and sometimes the conversation got a little heated.

The *New York Times* sent a reporter to cover the competition's first year.

By then, we saw which ArtPrize entries were in the running for the top prize. A top 25 list was updated regularly on the ArtPrize website. Some of us worried about what was on the list.

"This community is potentially giving a quarter of a million dollars to what is potentially a weak work of art," Kendall College Art professor Deborah Rockman told the *Times* reporter.

Was it an economic development tool? A cultural conversation starter? Or a radical new way to judge art? Would it bring life to a fledgling downtown? Would it lead us out of the rust belt and into the creative class economy?

Young Kim, *Salt & Earth,* 2009

Rockman, herself a trained artist, worried that only the biggest, most attention-grabbing works of art would stand a chance of winning the public's vote.

The story was a centerpiece on the front page of the *Times*' Art section.[1]

And here was both the promise and the problem of ArtPrize. The competition had the power to redefine the image of Grand Rapids. We were a city known for only two things: Gerald Ford and the furniture industry. That's if we were known at all. Events in Grand Rapids rarely made the national news. ArtPrize was making national news. We worried that if the wrong piece won the competition, it would confirm, rather than dispel, the old stodgy stereotypes about our city.

When we voted in ArtPrize, we didn't just vote for ourselves. We voted for our city, and how it would be seen by the rest of the world.

When the ArtPrize top 10 was announced, one piece left out was *Salt & Earth*, by North Carolina artist Young Kim. The piece consisted of a series of portraits silk-screened onto square piles of loose salt. It was haunting and beautiful. It had a devoted following among ArtPrize voters. Some ArtPrize voters. When *salt and earth* failed to make the top 10, admirers took to Twitter, using the hashtag #sorryyoungkim.

In the end, the $250,000 prize went to an artist from

Ran Ortner, *Open Water No. 24,* 2009.

Brooklyn named Ran Ortner, for *Open Water No. 24*, a photorealistic oil painting of turbulent waves reflecting an uncertain sky.

Even if it wasn't everyone's favorite, it was a piece that represented Grand Rapids.

Water had inspired the city's public art in the past, from Alexander Calder's *La Grande Vitesse* and Maya Lin's *Ecliptic*, to the downtown buildings that take the waves of the Grand River as design cues.

Ortner said he'd never been to Grand Rapids before ArtPrize. He'd never even heard of it. And he didn't know anything about the Grand River, or its role in the city's art history. That didn't stop us from seeing the river in his painting.

At the awards ceremony, there was also a surprise $5,000 prize given to Young Kim for *Salt & Earth*. Later, this idea to reward art that had failed to win

the public's vote would evolve into a new category of awards for ArtPrize. These awards would be decided not by popular vote, but by a selection of art professionals.

We had decided that ArtPrize couldn't just toss a hand-grenade into the arts establishment. There had to be a handshake. Otherwise, why would artists like Young Kim even agree to travel to our city and show their work?

The juried awards were put in place for ArtPrize's second year.

We braced for another big year. This time it was less of a surprise. We were ready. At the very least, restaurants promised they wouldn't run out of food.

And the crowds were bigger.

When the top 10 was announced, we swarmed to see each piece. Sometimes, we stood in line for hours. We were thousands of people in a mid-size Midwestern city waiting in line to see art. The Grand Rapids Art Museum, which had three pieces in the top 10 that year, had more

Left: Alexander Calder, *La Grande Vitesse*, 1969.

Above: Maya Lin, *Ecliptic*, 2001; photo: Balthazar Korab, Courtesy of the Frey Foundation.

visitors during the three weeks of ArtPrize than it had in the entire previous year.

GRAM also hosted the winner that year, an expansive and detailed pencil drawing by a local artist, Chris LaPorte.

In 2011, as ArtPrize entered its third year, we could feel how it had changed life in the city, not just during the three weeks of the competition, but year-round. Now, when business owners or developers announced new projects downtown, the goal was always to open in time for ArtPrize. When relatives or friends planned their visits, they planned them around ArtPrize.

We still didn't agree on the art, of course. Year three proved to be a particularly loaded year for conversations about ArtPrize. It was the year a religious piece would win the top prize.

The rest of the top 10 was once again dominated by large, attention-grabbing works of art.

"Unfortunately, overwhelmingly the art community is a little bit freaked out by the top ten," local artist Tommy Allen told Michigan Radio after the awards were announced that year. "But at the end of the day, if this is how the public voted, it's how they voted."[2]

The juried prizes had brought some attention to smaller, more challenging works of art. But those prizes were tiny compared to the $250,000 top prize decided by public vote. And if ArtPrize was a conversation, as Rick DeVos reiterated again and again, the professional arts community was feeling that its voice amounted to little more than a whisper, uttered in a crowded room.

Even with this growing tension, ArtPrize in 2011 was a huge success. The economic impact of ArtPrize that year was calculated at more than $15 million, double what it had been just two years before.

The competition could have kept going on the same path, growing the crowds and the economic benefits, while ignoring the concerns of the arts community.

Chris LaPorte, *Cavalry, American Officers, 1921*, 2010.

Instead, ArtPrize changed again.

In 2012, the juried awards would get bigger, from $7,000 to $20,000. And ArtPrize created a new award, the Juried Grand Prize, worth $100,000.

At the same time, the top prize for the public vote went down, from $250,000 to $200,000. Four years in, ArtPrize was fluid, still experimenting.

In 2012, the competition had many of the same contours we'd come to expect. Long lines, crowded streets. Art everywhere.

But this time, there were new visitors and new voices, well-known names from the world of art, here to have their say for the Juried Grand Prize.

None of these names was better known, and none of these voices were more listened to, than Jerry Saltz's, senior art critic for *New York Magazine.* If there is such a thing as a celebrity art critic, Saltz is it. He's been nominated for the Pulitzer Prize in criticism three times. He's been on a reality show. He's danced with Jay-Z.

Saltz had commented on ArtPrize before, in a *Wall Street Journal* article in 2010, when he called ArtPrize "terrifying and thrilling."[3]

His trip to Grand Rapids for ArtPrize in 2012 was captured in a short documentary film released online by the ArtPrize organization (www.artprize.org/film). In the film, Saltz is a chatty swashbuckler. He grabs random strangers to ask what they think of the art, then interrupts and adds on as new ideas come to him.

Back in the window-lit conference room at ArtPrize headquarters, Saltz declares to the camera, "This is one of the best art experiences I've ever had."

Saltz and the rest of the appointed panel of art experts saved their highest praise for SiTE:LAB, a venue that invited artists from around the world to reimagine spaces within the empty former home of the Grand Rapids Public Museum. In 2011, SiTE:LAB organizers had won a surprise juried award for best venue. In 2012, art hosted at SiTE:LAB won four of the six juried prize categories, including the $100,000 Juried Grand Prize.

The experts told us this wasn't just the best art at ArtPrize. It was some of the best art anywhere.

Design 99, *Displacement (13208 Klinger St.),* 2012.

"It is the BEST SPACE for artist-curated exhibitions I have seen in the United States for some time," Saltz declared on SiTE:LAB's Facebook page.

Not that any of this affected how most of us voted. The art at SiTE:LAB dominated the conversation, and the accolades, among art experts. But not a single piece from the venue reached the top 10 in public voting.

We had more voices. But our conversations did not merge.

In April of 2013, ArtPrize hired a new executive director. Christian Gaines was the first director of the organization to come from outside West Michigan, and he arrived with experience from the world of film festivals.

In an interview with Rapid Growth Media, Gaines talked about the separate worlds ArtPrize had managed to bring together, but not quite yet integrate. "There's sort of an exclusivity to contemporary art that makes people feel like they could not belong, and I don't think anyone wants that," Gaines said.[4]

ArtPrize began as a way to bring those other voices into the conversation. As the fifth year of the event approached, the focus was more on how to manage the collision between populist and professional ideas about art. In the fifth year, those ideas collided hard.

In coffee shops and cubicles, at restaurants and bus stops, in person and online, we talked about art. We talked about what we loved, what we hated. We argued.

ArtPrize had changed the conversation, and sometimes the conversation got a little heated.

The ArtPrize Awards, 2013; photo: T.J. Hamilton / Stellafly.

In 2013, the art professionals behind the juried prizes shared their shortlists for potential winners midway through the competition, as they had the year before. By the end of voting, there was zero overlap between the jurors' short lists and the public vote's top 25.

This duality, this tension, had come to define ArtPrize in a way. We knew, after five years, ArtPrize would not be just one thing. ArtPrize would be SiTE:LAB and Jerry Saltz. It would also be a 20-year-old's paper airplane project and an awful lot of dragon sculptures.

It was economic development and cultural engagement. It was messy. It was beautiful. It was crowded. It was ugly. It was inspiring.

In 2013, an estimated 450,000 people visited downtown Grand Rapids for ArtPrize.

We were not one.

We were 450,000 different ArtPrizes, every one completely different from the next.

———

The 2013 ArtPrize award ceremony was broadcast live in Grand Rapids. Local NBC affiliate WOOD TV8 ran a countdown clock as the ceremony's start time approached. The scene was meticulously staged inside a city-owned maintenance garage. Yellow and purple spotlights roved through the crowd as a band jammed on stage.

The first person to speak was Todd Herring, director of communications for ArtPrize, and the night's emcee. He air-drummed in time with the band as he strode to the podium, wearing a suit with yellow slacks and a purple bow tie.

"Tonight we will be awarding $560,000 in prizes," he said, to cheers.

Awards were announced. There were messages from sponsors and jurors. Christian Gaines offered thanks to the community and the ArtPrize staff.

Then, Gaines introduced Rick DeVos, a 31-year-old with a famous name, though it was now famous for another reason.

His hair: still unkempt. His suit: snappy and grey, with a black tie.

DeVos said that, after five years, one of the most frequent questions he still gets about ArtPrize is, "How is it going?"

"My answer is, of course, good," he said. But that clearly understates it.

"What other city has tens of thousands of people who would never go to an art museum, thinking about and engaging with art? What other city has tens of thousands of school children engaging with contemporary art in the way they do at ArtPrize? What other city bumps *Access Hollywood* and a football game to broadcast live coverage about art?" DeVos said, what's happened with ArtPrize is unprecedented, and still unpredictable.

"A lot of people wonder about the implications of ArtPrize," he said. "But there are simply too many things going on here that have never happened before to guess how it will all play out."

---

1. Micheline Maynard, "Eyes on the ArtPrize" (*New York Times*, 7 Oct. 2009).

2. Lindsey Smith, "ArtPrize 2011 winners; thrilled, controversial, bittersweet." *Michigan Radio*, 7 Oct. 2011.

3. Taylor Antrim, "Critical Mass." *Wall Street Journal Magazine*, 9 Sept. 2010.

4. J. Bennett Rylah, "Meet Christian Gaines, ArtPrize's New Executive Director." Rapid Growth 25 April 2013, at http://www.rapidgrowthmedia.com/features/04252013gaines.aspx (accessed 2-10-14).

Nathan Craven, *BAM POW* (detail), 2012

HOW TO ROLL A BALL DOWNHILL:
WHY ARTPRIZE IS SO SUCCESSFUL

Adam Lerner

first found out about ArtPrize in the spring of 2010 when I received a packet in the mail inviting me to give a lecture there. This was before ArtPrize achieved the international recognition it has today and I had never heard of it. And, as someone who frequents international biennial art exhibitions and art fairs, even before I read about its democratic selection process, I was suspicious of the enterprise. If it was so big, why had none of my colleagues mentioned it? What serious contemporary art program would have the word "prize" in the title? What international art could possibly originate in Grand Rapids, Michigan? I set the packet down and waited a few days before responding.

That was the snob in me. Even though I thought of myself as democratic-minded, as a museum director who spent ten years in a PhD program before working his way up from an assistant curator position, there was a part of me that was suspicious of things that came from outside the known art world. The events that I was accustomed to featured international artists and curators whose names I recognized. There were usually galleries from places like Berlin and London involved. ArtPrize simply felt different.

But the anti-snob in me was intrigued. Before I became a museum director, I actually ran an art center in a shopping district in the suburbs of Denver, a place that art-world snobs didn't care about one bit. So as much as the academically trained curator in me felt unsure about

ArtPrize, the experimental and egalitarian side of me was interested, even excited, to see what was in store. So, I accepted the invitation.

Early in my visit, ArtPrize put the snob in me to shame.

I began to grasp the power of ArtPrize on the plane from Denver to Grand Rapids. There was a guy, let's call him Mike, in his 20s sitting next to me in blue jeans and a flannel shirt, not the hipster kind. He told me he lived in the outskirts of Grand Rapids and he worked as a mechanic for an auto-racing outfit. I had no idea what that involved but I learned that in his world there was a lot of hard work, travel, and hope. This was in the midst of the economic malaise and it seemed as if he had to work hard chasing a relatively small amount of money. When I told him I was the director of an art museum, he asked if I was going to Grand Rapids for ArtPrize. He said that he had been the previous year and that he intended to go back this year as well. He told me what I should expect and what he liked about it. He was proud of his city and wasn't at all surprised that an art museum director from Denver would be flying out for the event.

That's when I first began to understand that ArtPrize was indeed different from all the other art events I attend. From everything I could tell, Mike was not among the usual demographic for art museum visitors. As much as we museum directors would like to have it otherwise, our core audience is made up of overeducated NPR listeners,

Improv Everywhere, *The Mp3 Experiment*, 2011.

much like ourselves. We believe we have to present blockbuster exhibitions like *King Tut* and *The Art of the Motorcycle* to be able to attract mainstream audiences from beyond the urban core. But ArtPrize demonstrated that guys like Mike are happy to look at landscape paintings and portrait sculptures by unknown artists.

What did ArtPrize offer that art museums did not?

When I arrived in downtown Grand Rapids, I saw a version of Mike's enthusiasm everywhere. The streets were filled with people gathered to look at all kinds of art and vote for their favorite ones. There was a line out the door of the Grand Rapids Art Museum. People were shuffling into coffee shops and restaurants to look at the art. The organization estimates that, over the course of less than three weeks, the event draws approximately 400,000 visitors to the city, with 40,000 people actively voting on art. By comparison, the international art fair Art Basel Miami Beach, attracts approximately 50,000 participants over its five days. And that's Miami Beach.

What is the attraction? It is simply not the art. If art in general were an attractor, then art museums across the country would not be staging massive exhibitions of Impressionist painting every year to draw visitors. It's not even the scale of the art on display that explains its draw. If the city had hosted a giant multi-venue art exhibition by selecting a large team of curators, it surely would have resulted in a significant event—if it were given the right amount of hype. It would have attracted audiences because events are eventful. But ArtPrize does not draw visitors through hype. Its magnetic pull draws an increasing number of visitors year after year without a humongous advertising budget.

ArtPrize draws people in a fundamentally different way than other big art exhibitions. Once it took hold, it acquired a natural centripetal force attracting viewers, more like Fourth of July fireworks displays or the Superbowl than an art event. It has become a part of the life of a city, akin to Mardi Gras of New Orleans or the Carnival of Brazil. It is one of those things that people come together to do because that's simply what they do periodically as a community. In a word, ArtPrize has managed to become something civic.

Unlike many European cities, which benefit from large public funding for the arts, American cities are rarely able to host large, civic art events that engage citizens at large. Museums, the primary agent of the organized presentation of art, have a strong tendency to draw people into buildings. By their nature, museums need to focus on their own preservation before they are able to care for the well-being of the city. Museums evaluate their success not by the ripple effects that they create around them, but by the number of the people who walk through their doors. ArtPrize differs from the museum

model because the domain that it cares about is not a building but the city.

The civic nature of ArtPrize recalls something lost in American history. Twenty-first century American society has largely abandoned its earlier aspirations to nurture anything that might be considered civic life. From that perspective, ArtPrize is an important historical development.

Structured as a widely inclusive competition, ArtPrize is so different from mainstream art institutions that it can only be appreciated by looking back to a time before those institutions were taken for granted. ArtPrize harkens back to a time when alternatives to the art museum were being seriously considered, reviving an early twentieth-century American belief that the highest function of art is to allow everyday people to express themselves in common. Seeing the potential for art far beyond the museum walls, American cultural leaders at the time looked to art as way of creating secular rituals to unify a diverse society.

The idea of creating art events on a civic scale emerged alongside the modern democratic project itself, emerging as an answer to the questions faced by newly modernizing nations. In a society that is no longer united around the spectacles of the monarch, what spectacles will it create? In a society where religion is a private matter, what are the rituals that bind communities?

These questions might seem far afield from the issue at hand but these are precisely the issues in the air at the founding of the very first art museum, the Louvre, in 1793. It was inaugurated after the French Revolution as part of a citywide festival celebrating the first anniversary of the founding of the republic. The opening of the museum was the culmination of a parade where temporary statues representing liberty and fraternity were carried through the streets. Therefore, at the very founding of the museum concept, people understood their participation in the museum as part of their involvement in a civic and national event.[1]

When the Swiss philosopher Jean-Jacques Rousseau, whose ideas largely inspired the festival for the opening of the Louvre, was asked to give his advice on the formation an independent government of Poland, he recommended the creation of art festivals and games. He looked back in history and was particularly interested in the way that games kept the people of Sparta united and spirited. He looked at ancient Greece where the poems of Homer were read in front of the entire nation assembled. Importantly, Rousseau did not want art to be separated from civic life and hated that theater

> The civic nature of ArtPrize recalls something lost in American history. Twenty-first century American society has largely abandoned its earlier aspirations to nurture anything that might be considered civic life. From that perspective, ArtPrize is an important historical development.

Community singing event, Powderhorn Park, Minneapolis, n.d.
Courtesy of Hennepin Public Library Special Collections.

had become an event confined to designated buildings accessible only to ticket-holders. He wanted the stage to be the civic arena itself, for people to gather in the commons and experience art together.[2] In short, with his emphasis on arts festivals, contests, and public gatherings, Rousseau's suggestions for the activities of a free society were actually quite similar to the principles underlying ArtPrize.

Despite its affinity with European political thought, ArtPrize belongs to a long tradition of American efforts to use art to cultivate civil life. In the early twentieth century, museums vied with other institutions for the appropriate art institution for a democratic nation. At its root, the question came down to whether the United States should embrace elevated ideas of art from Europe or invent new, inclusive formats. While this early conflict

is largely forgotten today, it is crucial for understanding the importance of ArtPrize as an alternative to the museum model of culture.

I like to think about the struggle over the civic function of culture in early twentieth-century America as a conflict between the Lincoln Memorial (1914–1922) and Mount Rushmore (1927–1941). The Lincoln Memorial, filled with symbolism and references to the tradition of Western art from Ancient Greece, represents an idea of culture as a product of refined taste. The high staircase alone could be seen to represent the notion of cultural uplift embodied in the memorial, an idea that permeates museum culture as well. By contrast, Mount Rushmore,

rooted in the earth, represented an organic idea of culture as a democratic expression of the people. In Mount Rushmore, sculptor Gutzon Borglum sought to create a monument people could understand without feeling as if they needed to know art history, a monument that very clearly said "America" without hiding any obscure and noble messages.[3] Early twentieth-century America allowed for the coexistence of the Lincoln Memorial and Mount Rushmore.

The organic notion of culture symbolized by Mount Rushmore took many forms in American society in the early twentieth century. The most striking of these efforts was the "community singing" movement. Led by Harry Barnhart, this movement swept the nation from 1914 to the early 1920s. Barnhart, who was virtually a household name at the time, staged events where tens of thousands of people gathered in parks to sing popular songs. Harry Barnhart and his cohort didn't consider this a popular leisure activity. It was not just amusement. It was talked about as having the potential to transform civic life. As hokey as it seems to us today, at the time community singing was seen as an alternative to the museum model of art, an approach that allowed for an entire community to express itself in producing a work of art together.[4]

Similar to the Community Singing movement, in the pageantry movement, quasi-famous pageant directors traveled around the country organizing dramatic events that allowed communities to tell their own history in a way that Rousseau would appreciate. One of the most famous pageant leaders, Percy MacKaye, organized the Pageant and Masque of Saint Louis in 1914 with a cast of 7,000 and an audience of up to 100,000. One hundred years ago, there was the feeling that maybe this emerging powerhouse of a nation would express itself through activities that allowed the citizens themselves to participate in expressing the art of their time.[5]

It is important to contextualize ArtPrize within the history of participatory art aspirations in the United States because people in positions like mine have a tendency to think that the museum model has always been the only legitimate one. Because they were largely ephemeral events, with no lasting structures, it is easy to forget the institutions that coincided with the emergence of art museums in America, institutions that sought new ways of incorporating art into civic life. Even though museum culture predominated for much of the twentieth century, the natural landscape of culture in the United States is a dualistic one, combining both elevated and participatory art institutions.

Though ArtPrize revives a long-dormant tradition, it does so in an entirely twenty-first century way. Its inventiveness is not based on technology, though its advanced systems facilitate its widespread participation. Rather, the essential innovation of ArtPrize lies in marrying the art exhibition with the contest format. The

competitive element of ArtPrize is the key to differentiating between ArtPrize and traditional art museums. In many ways, the principles embodied in museums are not very far from the ideals motivating ArtPrize. As alluded to above, the Louvre was conceived out of an interest in universal human values, an idea foundational to modern thought. The universal element of the museum is rooted in the idea that art expresses something we all share, something about what it means to be human. The difference between the museum concept and ArtPrize begins to emerge not in the theory, since these are both fundamentally democratic, but in the way that theory is enacted. Historically, museums have thought of themselves as taking on the qualities of the art in their care, valuing themselves by what they are, not what they do. That is why, as much as museums since the eighteenth century have described themselves as places of uplift and education, they have always been vague about the actual mechanisms through which they engage their visitors. Universities, by contrast, because they originated with monastic teaching, are very clear about their reliance on the mechanism of classroom learning. More like universities than museums, at its conception ArtPrize has a built-in mechanism for participation, one that is essential to its identity.

ArtPrize adopted the idea of voting because, simply put, that's how people like to be involved in things. There is a reason that *American Idol* is one of the most successful shows in the history of American television. When I consciously vote for one contestant among many, I more actively engage my faculty of judgment than if I were a more passive spectator. Neuroscientists refer to this process as integration, building a connection between sense perception and other faculties of the mind. And, if

the competition has multiple iterations, then I become a player in its unfolding drama. ArtPrize is based on that form of engagement. Whereas the museum was created as an edifice to express universal human values, ArtPrize created the competition format as an engine to enable universal participation.

This is not to say that the art museum has no drivers for participation. It is to say that those drivers are considered outside of its essence. In practice, major art museums outside of tourist destinations generally drive visitation by presenting familiar subjects supported by massive publicity campaigns. The reason that van Gogh, Picasso, and Warhol are continually given museum exhibitions is that celebrity is the primary audience driver. Regardless of how successful the museum is in attracting visitors, it always brings them through expensive campaigns. Museums continually push the ball uphill.

The continual campaign for visitors is often a cause of tension in museums themselves. I was recently asked to review applications by art museum curators competing to participate in an exclusive professional development program. Reading through dozens of applications, I was shocked at the widespread level of discontent among art museum curators at large institutions. These highly educated individuals, who value themselves for their refined historical expertise and connoisseurship, find themselves in conflict with the leaders of their institutions, who they often see as too reliant on crowd-pleasing exhibitions. Fundamentally divided between great art and great audience, art museums today continually bear

> Whereas the museum was created as an edifice to express universal human values, ArtPrize created the competition format as an engine to enable universal participation.

the consequences of the fact that their method for engaging audiences is not written into their DNA.

By contrast, ArtPrize's mechanism for engaging audiences is essential to its concept. It is Art*Prize* afterall.

ArtPrize engages visitors because it offers something appropriate to a society that increasingly pursues its highest ambitions through games. Games are everywhere drivers of participation. The most famous example of the use of the game model is X Prize, which offers large cash prizes to encourage innovation. Founded in 1994 by Peter Diamandis, the first X Prize awarded $10 million to the first private enterprise to launch a manned spacecraft into space twice within two weeks. Today, the X Prize Foundation not only awards several prizes on that scale, but also includes $30 million in prizes for private enterprises that can operate a rover on the surface of the moon. For any competitor, the cost of participating will inevitably exceed the prize but the prize sets up the challenge. This concept of "incentivized competition" has spread widely. In 2010, 57,000 gamers participated in an online, multi-player game involving the computational challenge of folding proteins.[6] In her book *Reality Is Broken: Why Games Make Us Better and How They Can Change the World*, Jane McGonical argues for games as a way of solving everything from personal to global problems. Whereas the entire history of modern capitalism is based on the power of competition, we are only recently coming to understand just how powerful the force of competition can be. Even with the ubiquity of sports competition throughout the world, it took the stupendous rise of video games (for some reason) for us to realize that winning is a motivator in itself, even without any material gain.

ArtPrize is uniquely able to escape the contradictions of the art museum, in part because it was conceived on a whiteboard. A few smart people stood around asking what kind of cultural event they could create that would generate civic participation. Created like a start-up, it

had no preconceived loyalties, except to popular participation and visitation to downtown Grand Rapids. It is instructive that Rick DeVos originally assembled the group that would develop ArtPrize to create a citywide independent film festival in Grand Rapids. When the idea didn't pan out because of widespread competition in the film festival arena, they developed the concept focused on the visual arts.

Because ArtPrize was developed free of any institutional loyalties or professional stakes, it represents the values and interests of our time. It not only embodies democratic ideals but also addresses the problem of how to realize them. ArtPrize belongs to the world where leaders ask the question: What will excite people about participating? And they figure out a way to do that.

That's when the ball rolls downhill.

---

1. Andrew McClellan, *The Art Museum from Boullée to Bilbao* (Berkeley: University of California Press, 2008); Dorinda Outram, *The Body and the French Revolution: Sex, Class, and Political Culture* (New Haven: Yale University Press, 1989).

2. Jean-Jacques Rousseau, "Considerations on the Government of Poland," in *Jean-Jacques Rousseau: The Social Contract and Other Later Political Writings* (Cambridge, UK: Cambridge University Press, 1997 [1772]), 177–260.

3. Adam J. Lerner, Gutzon Borglum's "Conception," *American Art*, Vol. 12, no. 2 (Summer 1998), 70.

4. Very little has been written about the Community Singing movement. The best source focuses on Claude Bragdon, the visionary architect who designed the lighting for the events. See Jonathan Massey, *Crystal and Arabesque: Claude Bragdon, Ornament, and Modern Architecture* (Pittsburgh: University of Pittsburgh Press, 2009).

5. David Glassberg, *American Historical Pageantry: The Uses of Tradition in the Early Twentieth Century* (Chapel Hill: The University of North Carolina Press, 1990).

6. Jane McGonigal, "Be a Gamer, Save the World," *Wall Street Journal*, January 22, 2011. http://online.wsj.com/article/SB1 0001424052748704590704576092460302990884.html (accessed 9-27-13).

I'm astounded by the potential for social networking, community involvement, and the expanded view of the role of art. ArtPrize will excite the world, and the world will look at our city differently because of it.

— GRAND RAPIDS MAYOR GEORGE HEARTWELL, APRIL 23, 2009

It is increasingly important to find new ways to engage people, especially young people, in the arts. ArtPrize is a dynamic and creative way to use technology to engage people of all ages.

— MICHAEL KAISER, PRESIDENT, KENNEDY CENTER FOR THE PERFORMING ARTS IN WASHINGTON, DC

It does impact me to walk into a coffee shop or a small restaurant or a museum and to see that the entries are from all walks of life. I think that this notion that art is for everyone, or can be for everyone, and made by everyone needs to be reinforced.

— MEL CHIN, ARTIST, 2013 JUROR

Grand Rapids transforms into an open playing field where anyone can find a voice in the conversation about what art is and why it matters.

— JOHN MILLER, *THE WALL STREET JOURNAL*

When you put a frame around something, it suddenly becomes art. . . . It's seen in a different light. ArtPrize puts a frame around three square miles of Grand Rapids and turns this place into something strange, magical, and wonderful.

— DR. DAVID ROSEN, PRESIDENT, KENDALL COLLEGE OF ART AND DESIGN OF FERRIS STATE UNIVERSITY

ArtPrize provides a happy marriage between a general public and an exclusive art world event.

— *HUFFINGTON POST*

During ArtPrize people have the sense that it's theirs, the art, the event, and that they are OK to have an opinion, that they are allowed to look, and allowed to experience, and to really enter a dialogue with a work of art—even if they don't have a lot of background about where they should begin with that.

— KEVIN BUIST, ARTPRIZE DIRECTOR OF EXHIBITIONS

Beili Liu, *Lure/Wave*, 2010

2009

ARTPRIZE 2009 WINNERS

First Place: Ran Ortner, *Open Water No. 24*

Second Place: Tracy Van Duinen, Cory Van Duinen, Todd Osborne, *Imagine That!*

Third Place: Eric Daigh, *Portraits*

Fourth Place: David Lubbers, *The Grand Dance*

Fifth Place: Bill Secunda, *Moose*

Sixth Place: Nessie Project (Thomas Birks, Richard App, Joachim Jensen, David Valdiserri), *Nessie on the Grand*

Seventh Place: John Douglas Powers, *Field of Reeds*

Eighth Place: Sarah Grant, *The Furniture City Sets the Table for the World of Art*

Ninth Place: Jason Hackenwerth, *Ecstasy of the Scarlet Empress*

Tenth Place: Michael Westra, *Winddancer 2*

Curator's Choice Award: Young Kim, *Salt & Earth*

Sustainability Award: Scott Hessels, *The Image Mill: Sustainable Cinema #1*

Jason Hackenwerth, *Ecstasy of The Scarlet Empress*, 2009

Terrence Karpowicz, *Pettite Passe,* 2009

The goal of ArtPrize is not to laude the artist who can distill the perfect average of public opinion. The goal is to encourage a vigorous and sincere debate with art on a massive scale. If people who come to ArtPrize continue to talk about it years after the art is gone, that is arguably more enduring than one public work people walk by every day and rarely consider.

—KEVIN BUIST, MAY 22, 2009

Tracy Van Duinen, Corey Van Duinen, Todd Osborne, *Imagine That!*, 2009

The Blue Bridge and Grand River with (left) Plamen
Yordanov, *Infinity (Double Möbius Strip)*, 2009; (foreground) Nessie
Project, *Nessie on the Grand*, 2009; and (on top of bridge) Sarah
Grant, *The Furniture City Sets the Table for the World of Art*, 2009.

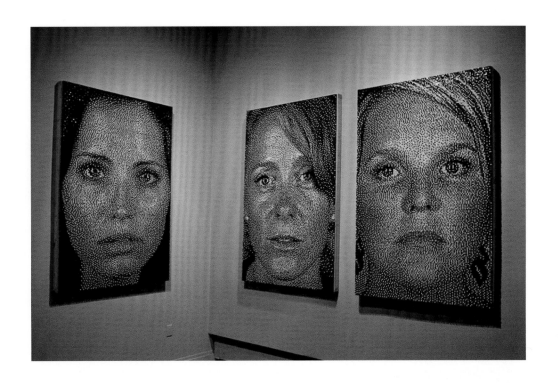

Opposite: Bill Secunda, *Moose*, 2009. Above: Eric Daigh, *Portraits*, 2009 (and detail).

The parking lot of The B.O.B., including Thomas Aitken, *Car Chase,* 2009

This is a bit of an art revolution. It will be exciting to see a city use its downtown area as an art gallery to share with the world.

—JEFF SPECK, FORMER DIRECTOR OF DESIGN, NATIONAL ENDOWMENT FOR THE ARTS, APRIL 23, 2009

The Blue Bridge, 2009

John Douglas Powers, *Field of Reeds,* 2009

From left to right: Deborah Adams Doering, *Code for the Grand River, Grand Rapids_09*, 2009; photo: Terry Johnston. Stafford Smith, Ritsu Katsumata, *Fearscape* (detail), 2009; photo: Terry Johnston. Aaron Heideman, *The Man in a Van Project*, 2009; photo: Terry Johnston. Scott Hessels, *The Image Mill: Sustainable Cinema #1*, 2009.

This is a city with a certain history with art, which is not irrelevant, and it's very particular. There's a story of Grand Rapids in the state of Michigan. There's a story of Grand Rapids in itself. And [ArtPrize] could leap ahead or at least find its own solid ground within, if you will, the high art world that we participate in, if it kept that really thoughtful and deep engagement.

—MARY JANE JACOB, PROFESSOR AND EXECUTIVE DIRECTOR OF EXHIBITIONS AND EXHIBITION STUDIES, SCHOOL OF THE ART INSTITUTE OF CHICAGO, 2009 ARTPRIZE GUEST LECTURER

Jason Hackenwerth, *Ecstasy of The Scarlet Empress*, 2009

2013 Juror Eva Franch i Gilabert discusses Urban Space nominees.

ABOUT THE JURORS

Kevin Buist

ArtPrize began with a singular emphasis on the public vote. The largest art prize in the world, decided by anyone who came to look, was key to its radical simplicity. While the 2009 ArtPrize Awards did include two small juried prizes, one of which was a surprise, it wasn't until 2010 that we built a series of juried prizes into the architecture of the event.

We recognized the importance of giving accolades to work that really deserved acknowledgment, but that wasn't getting traction in the public vote. It was also a way to market the registration process to artists who were doing challenging and inventive work, but who were thinking that their work wouldn't connect with a wide enough public audience to get one of the top 10 prizes. We wanted artists who were making thought-provoking work to have a compelling reason to enter as well. We added six prizes based on categories for $5,000 each, which was raised to $7,000 the following year.

Going into the 2012 event we decided that we needed to step up the emphasis on the juried awards. We raised the category award amounts from $7,000 each to $20,000, and, most significantly, we added the Juried Grand Prize at $100,000. At the same time, the amount of public vote prizes was reduced slightly. Shifting the structure of the prizes so that the public vote and juried processes are both emphasized was a way of highlighting the diversity of ways we experience and analyze art. The critical conversation that is spurred by the mingling of these approaches lies at the core of our mission.

When I began the work of selecting the jurors for the first Juried Grand Prize in 2012, I was thinking, *What happens when you take a typical mid-sized town and shoot it full of massive amounts of art and people and prize money for a couple of weeks?* I began to think about who is working at the intersection of art, cities, and populism. Who had interesting things to say within the context of a temporary, urban-focused, gamelike international art exhibition? Our professional jurors—working artists, curators, critics, and arts administrators from the national and international art communities—are leaders in these shifting fields. The artists they select for prizes are those who do remarkable things with the audience, spaces, and energy that ArtPrize provides.

2010

POPULAR VOTE

First Place: Chris LaPorte, *Cavalry, American Officers, 1921*

Second Place: Mia Tavonatti, *Svelata*

Third Place: Beili Liu, *Lure/Wave, Grand Rapids*

Fourth Place: Paul Baliker, *A Matter of Time*

Fifth Place: David Spriggs, *Vision*

Sixth Place: Wander Martich, *Helping Mom One Penny at a Time*

Seventh Place: Bill Secunda, *Dancing with Lions*

Eighth Place: Young Kim, *Salt & Earth (Garden for Patricia)*

Ninth Place: Thomas Birks and Joachim Jensen, *SteamPig*

Tenth Place: Fredrick Prescott, *Elephant Walk*

JURIED PRIZES

2-D Work: Andrew Lewis Doak and Adrian Clark Hatfield, *Garden Party*

3-D Work: Mark Wentzel, *XLoungeSeries*

Time/Performance-Based Work: Yoni Goldstein, *The Jettisoned*

Best Use of Urban Space: Rick Beerhorst, Rose Beerhorst, Andre Beaumont, and Mike Hoyte, *Plan B*

International Award: Alex Schweder La, *Evaporative Buildings*

Sustainability Award: Paul Baliker, *A Matter of Time*

Alex Schweder La, *Evaporative Buildings*, 2009

Joshua Kirsch, *Sympathetic Resonance,* 2010; photo: Vince Dudzinski.

Involvement has increased significantly from one year to the next not just in the numbers of people who were voting … but there's also the corporate support, the commercial support, the city support, the kinds of enthusiasm in the city for it. Clearly they've embraced it. … I mean, in the end it's about energizing the city in difficult times.

—JAMES CUNO, PRESIDENT AND CEO, J. PAUL GETTY TRUST

Young Kim, *Salt & Earth (Garden for Patricia)*, 2010

Janice Arnold, *Chroma Passage*, 2010

Children visit the Urban Institute for Contemporary Arts (UICA), 2010

Sometimes art is not the object itself, it's the time that it produces for us, the time to see . . . The encounter . . .

—EVA FRANCH GILABERT, DIRECTOR AND CURATOR, STOREFRONT FOR ART AND ARCHITECTURE, NYC, 2013 JUROR

Kathy Stecko, *Dreamscape,* 2010

What was really important to me, from the moment I arrived, was this kind of public acceptance, and I'm not only talking about the audience. I was happily surprised by the community here; from art museums and public spaces to corporate offices to big buildings, everybody is participating one way or another. This is a very unique situation. For starters usually, it is very difficult to get permission to do this. Here it seems that everyone is ready to facilitate ArtPrize, eager to experiment, willing to turn their lobbies and their entrance areas into exhibition halls. The whole town is embracing the event.
—XENIA KALPAKTSOGLOU, CO-DIRECTOR, ATHENS BIENNALE, AND 3-D AWARD JUROR, 2010

Robert Bose, *Balloon Chain,* 2010

Woody Jones, *Where do you get those ideas?*, 2010

Parking lot of The B.O.B., including *SteamPig*, by Thomas Birks and Joachim Jensen. 2010.

Well, you cannot help but notice the volume of people, right? It's kind of like this astonishing cross between a sort of *Skulptur Projekte Münster* and *Burning Man.* There's this exuberant community outpouring and enthusiasm in the downtown area.

— TOM ECCLES, EXECUTIVE DIRECTOR, CENTER FOR CURATORIAL STUDIES, BARD COLLEGE, ARTPRIZE 2010 GUEST SPEAKER

Rod Klingelhofer, *The Grand Mean,* 2010

Mark Wentzel, *XLounge Series*, 2010

2011

POPULAR VOTE

First Place: Mia Tavonatti, *Crucifixion*

Second Place: Tracy Van Duinen, Todd Osborne, Phil Shuster, *Metaphorest*

Third Place: Lynda Cole, *Rain*

Fourth Place: Sunti Pichetchaiyakul, *President Gerald Ford Visits ArtPrize*

Fifth Place: Ritch Branstrom, *Rusty: A Sense of Direction/Self Portrait*

Sixth Place: Llew (Doc) Tilma, *Grizzlies on the Ford*

Seventh Place: Laura Alexander, *The Tempest II*

Eighth Place: Paul Baliker, *Ocean Exodus*

Ninth Place: Robert Shangle, *Under Construction*

Tenth Place: Bill Secunda, *Mantis Dreaming*

JURIED PRIZES

2-D Work: Mimi Kato, *One Ordinary Day of an Ordinary Town*

3-D Work: Michelle Brody, *Nature Preserve*

Time/Performance-Based Work: Caroline Young, *Remember:Replay:Repeat*

Best Use of Urban Space: Catie Newell, *Salvaged Landscape*

Outstanding Venue: SiTE:LAB + U of M School of Art & Design

International Award: Shinji Turner-Yamamoto, *DISAPPEARANCES: An Eternal Journey*

Sustainability Award: Laura Milkins, *Walking Home: Stories from the Desert to the Great Lakes*

Shinji Turner-Yamamoto, *DISAPPEARANCES: An Eternal Journey*, 2011

Above: Evertt Beidler, *Progressive Movement(s)*, 2011. Opposite: Shawn Smith, *Re-Things*, 2011; photo: Vince Dudzinski.

Saul Gray-Hildenbrand, *It Is Lovely This Time of Year*, 2011, photo: Vince Dudzinski.

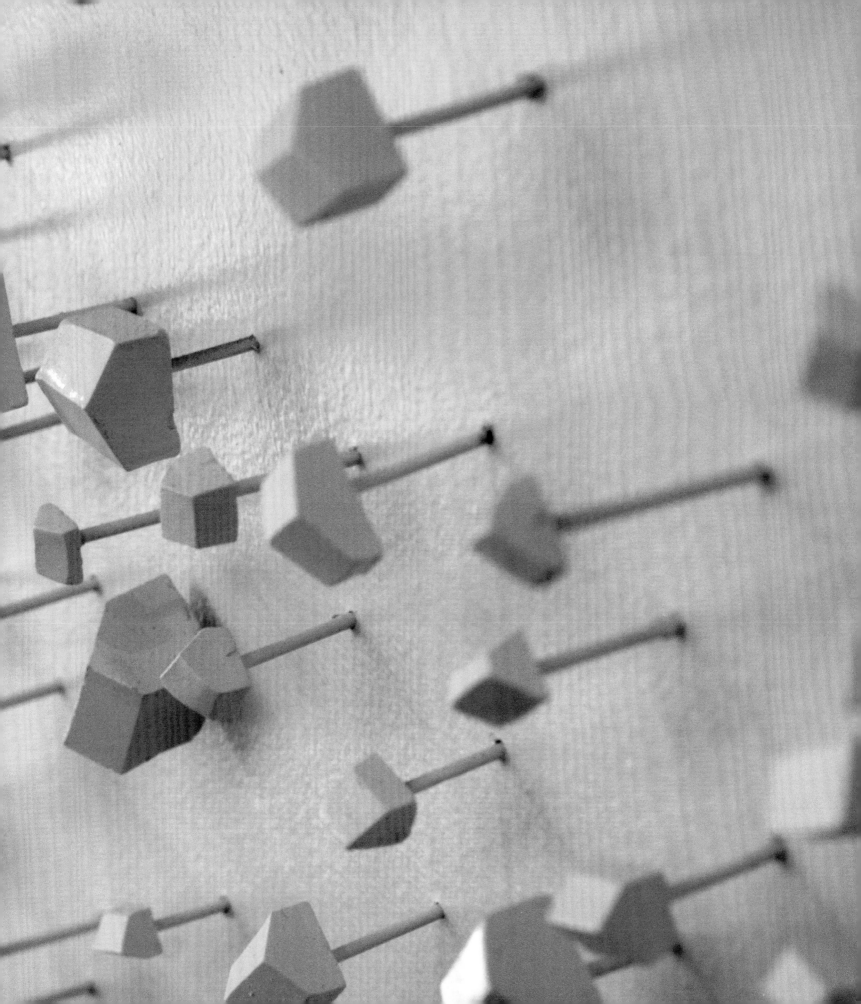

What's fascinating to me about ArtPrize is how it is a hybrid of several traditions in the art world that you wouldn't think would naturally go together. That's one.

Number two, it's like a giant art street fair. You know, the biggest one you've ever been to, and instead of having 160 booths, you have 1,600 individuals plastered all over town. So instead of making a little art ghetto that's four blocks long and has those God-awful booths, weird food for sale and all that, here, this whole side of the town becomes the booth.

—REED KROLOFF, DIRECTOR, CRANBROOK ACADEMY OF ART AND ART MUSEUM, 2011 ARTPRIZE URBAN SPACE AWARD JUROR

The Screwed Arts Collective, 2011
photo: Vince Dudzinski

Opposite page: Llew (Doc) Tilma, *Grizzlies on the Ford*, 2011. Above: Ritch Branstrom, *Rusty: A Sense of Direction/Self Portrait*, 2011.

Mia Tavonatti, *Crucifixion*, 2011

A new economic impact study was released this morning by Experience Grand Rapids, the region's convention and visitors bureau. The study, conducted by the Anderson Economic Group, reveals that the 2011 ArtPrize event added $15.4 million to the Grand Rapids/Kent County economy, attracted more than 320,000 visitors, and created more than 200 new jobs during its 19 days.

—BRIAN BURCH, ARTPRIZE BLOG, DECEMBER 20, 2011

Above: Students participate in a flashmob performance, 2011; photo: Vince Dudzinski. Opposite: Lorri Acott, *Conversation with Myself*, 2011.

Above: Jonathan Brilliant, *Have Sticks Will Travel*, 2011. Opposite: Mark Rumsey, *The Sky Is Not Falling*, 2011; photo: Vince Dudzinski.

2012

POPULAR VOTE

First Place: Adonna Khare, *Elephants*

Second Place: Martijn van Wagtendonk, *Song of Lift*

Third Place: Frits Hoendervanger, *Rebirth of Spring*

Fourth Place: Richard Morse, *Stick-to-it-ive-ness: Unwavering Pertinacity; Perseverance*

Fifth Place: Mark Carpenter and Dan Johnson, *Lights in the Night*

Sixth Place: Dan Heffron, *Life in Wood*

Seventh Place: Kumi Yamashita, *Origami*

Eighth Place: Artistry of Wildlife (Dennis Harris, Andrew Harris, Joseph Miles, Jamie Outman, Paul Thompson), *The Chase*

Ninth Place: Sandra Bryant, *Return to Eden*

Tenth Place: Chris LaPorte, *City Band*

JURIED PRIZES

Juried Grand Prize: Design 99 (Gina Reichert and Mitch Cope), *Displacement (13208 Klinger St.)*

2-D Work: Alois Kronschlager, *Habitat*

3-D Work: ABCD 83 (David Cuesta, Anthony Lewellen, Chris Silva, Brian Steckel), *More or Less*

Time/Performance-Based Work: Complex Movements (Wesley Taylor, Waajeed, Invincible, Tiff Massey, AJ Manoulian, Carlos Garcia), *Three Phases*

Best Use of Urban Space: Dale Rogers, *Flight*

Outstanding Venue: SiTE:LAB at 54 Jefferson

Kumi Yamashita, *Origami*, 2012

If everybody likes something, it's terrible—except here. It's defying the art world.

—JOHN WATERS, FILMMAKER, ARTPRIZE GUEST SPEAKER, 2012

Above: Adonna Khare creating her work *Elephants*, 2012. Courtesy of Bill Vriesema. John Waters speaking at ArtPrize, 2012. Opposite: Mike Simi, *Mr. Weekend*, 2012.

Scott Naylor, *Wave of Waves,* 2012

Above: Virginia Kistler, *Chiaroscuro,* 2012. Opposite: Mark Rumsey, *Deshabille (Paper Chain),* 2012.

I came not knowing what I was going to see. . . .
I've been blown away. . . . This is one of the best
art experiences I've ever had.

**—JERRY SALTZ, SENIOR ART CRITIC, *NEW YORK MAGAZINE*,
   2012 JUROR**

Opposite: Mark Carpenter and Dan Johnson, *Lights in the Night*, 2012.
Above: Eames House of Cards Education Days installation, 2012.

It's a call to the country, to land on Grand Rapids. ArtPrize got these 1500 plus participants to land on the website, to go through this dating ritual of object to space, and then those things spill out. . . . Whole senior facilities, whole elementary schools could go and think about works of art and judge them. It was amazing.

—**THEASTER GATES, ARTIST, DIRECTOR, ART AND PUBLIC LIFE, UNIVERSITY OF CHICAGO, 2012 JUROR**

Above: ABCD 83, *More or Less,* 2012. Opposite: Children participate in an Education Days program, 2012.

Above: Design 99, *Displacement (13208 Klinger St.)*, 2012. Opposite: Alois Kronschlaeger, *Habitat*, 2012; photo: Marc Lins.

Eighty-five percent of the art I see in Chelsea is not that good. Eighty-five percent of the work I saw in ArtPrize maybe isn't my favorite work, but my eighty-five percent is completely different than the eighty-five percent you found that's not that interesting to you. So that fifteen percent overlap where that happens is a remarkable place.

—JERRY SALTZ, SENIOR ART CRITIC, *NEW YORK MAGAZINE*, 2012 JUROR

Martijn van Wagtendonk, *Song of Lift*, 2012

2013

ARTPRIZE 2013 WINNERS

POPULAR VOTE

First Place: Ann Loveless, *Sleeping Bear Dune Lakeshore*

Second Place: Anni Crouter, *Polar Expressed*

Third Place: Andy Sacksteder, *Uplifting*

Fourth Place: Paul Baliker, *Dancing with Mother Nature*

Fifth Place: Jason Gamrath, *Botanical Exotica a Monumental Collection of the Rare Beautiful*

Sixth Place: Benjamin Gazsi, *Earth Giant*

Seventh Place: Robin Protz, *Myth-or-Logic*

Eighth Place: Fraser Smith, *Finding Beauty in Bad Things: Porcelain Vine*

Ninth Place: Michael Gard, *Taking Flight*

Tenth Place: Nick Jakubiak, *Tired Pandas*

JURIED PRIZES

Juried Grand Prize: Carlos Bunga, *Ecosystem*

2-D Work: Kyle Staver, *Europa and the Flying Fish*

3-D Work: Kevin Cooley and Phillip Andrew Lewis, *Through the Skies for You*

Best Use of Urban Space: JD Urban, *United.States: An Everydaypeople Project*

Time/Performance-Based Work: Shahzia Sikander, *The Last Post*

Outstanding Venue: Kendall College of Art and Design of Ferris State University

Robin Protz, *Myth-or-Logic*, 2013

Within the image (informational panel):
- 400 hours to complete four panels
- 18,000 yards of thread
- 50 yards of fusible web
- 75 yards of fabric
- Photo transfer birch tree onto fabric
- All machine Handi-Quilter (no hand sewing!)
- Long arm quilted on an Avante 18
- Vantage point is along Platte Bay on Lake Michigan in Benzie County

ArtPrize's real difference isn't cash. It's the event's unusual and daring ability to completely democratize the process of artistic judgment.
— *TIME* MAGAZINE

Above: Ann Loveless, *Sleeping Bear Dune Lakeshore,* 2013. Opposite: detail.

ArtPrize is all about audiences discovering great art, but while doing that we're also exploring a vibrant Grand Rapids, looking and lingering and yielding to the experiences waiting for us in Ah-Nab-Awen Park, on the Blue Bridge, in Rosa Parks Circle, up the street and around the corner of this remarkable city.
—CHRISTIAN GAINES, EXECUTIVE DIRECTOR, ARTPRIZE, 2013

Above and opposite: Mark Tucker, *FoolMoon GrandRapids,* 2013

Experience Grand Rapids, the official destination marketing organization for Kent County, released a study by East Lansing–based Anderson Economic Group that reveals ArtPrize 2013 added $22 million to the local economy, attracted more than 380,400 attendees, and created 253 jobs.
—EXPERIENCE GRAND RAPIDS, 2014

Above: Lauren Cotton, *Meridian*, 2013. Opposite: Mark Dean Veca, *Year of the Snake*, 2013.

Carlos Bunga, *Ecosystem*, 2013

Below: Charles Matson Lume, *The World's an Untranslatable Language II (for Charles Wright)*, 2013. Opposite: Daniel Arsham, *Watching,* 2013.

We're seeing such an explosion of experimentation in terms of artistic practice. . . . My primary interest here is that artists really are participating in the important ideas of our time, helping to shape consciousness toward a better collective future.

—ANNE PASTERNAK, PRESIDENT AND ARTISTIC DIRECTOR, CREATIVE TIME, 2013 ARTPRIZE JUROR

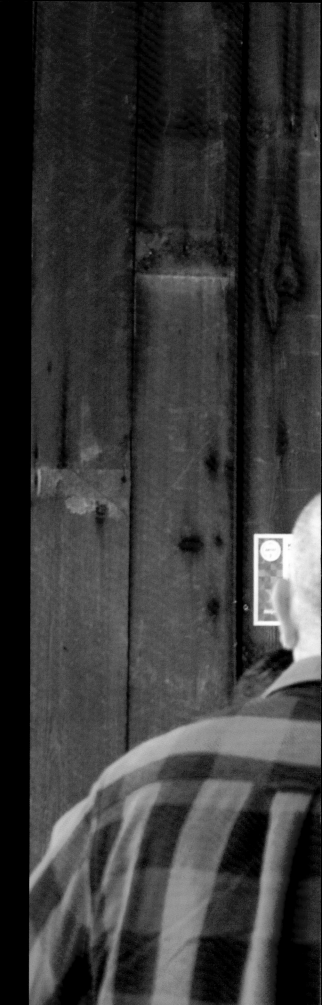

Kyle Staver, *Europa and the Flying Fish*, 2013

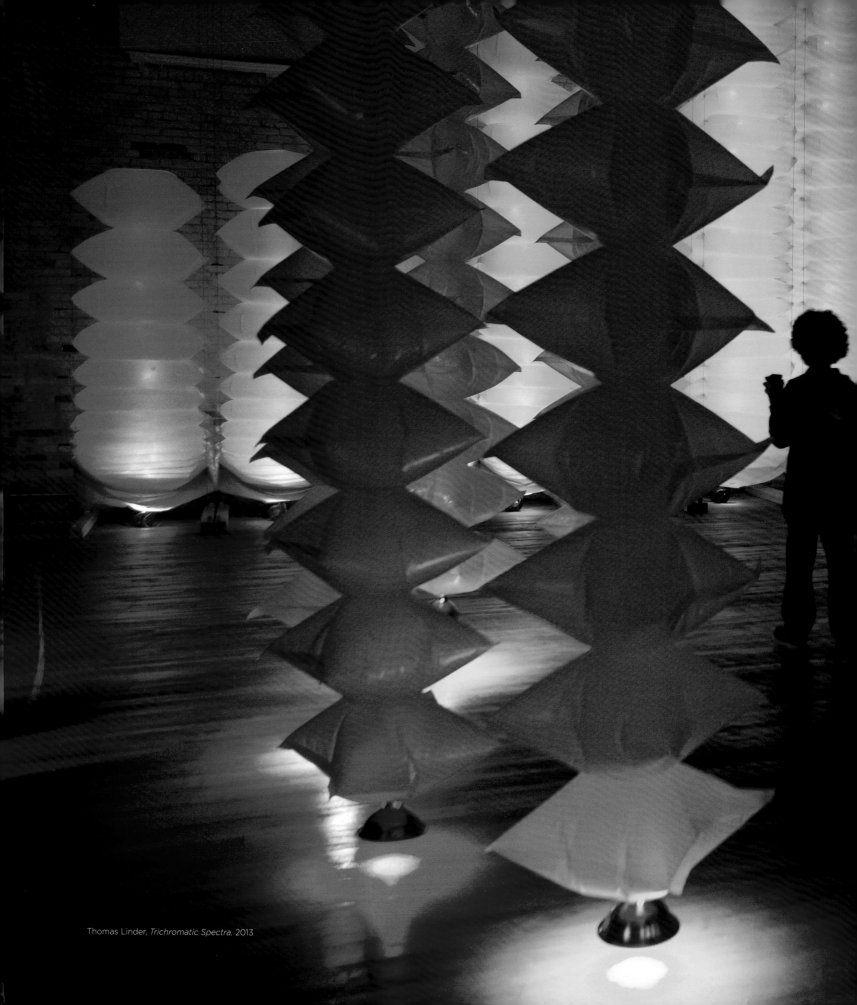

Thomas Linder, *Trichromatic Spectra*, 2013

ARTPRIZE JURORS 2010–2013

2010

2D

Patricia Phillips, Dean of Graduate Studies, Rhode Island School of Design

3D

Xenia Kalpaktsoglou, Curator and Co-director of Athens Biennale, Athens, Greece

TIME-BASED

Judith Barry, Director of the MFA Program, Art Institute of Boston

URBAN SPACE

Jeff Speck, Architect and City Planner, Washington, DC

INTERNATIONAL

Brett Colley, Associate Professor of Art, Grand Valley State University, Allendale, MI

David Greenwood, Professor of Sculpture and Functional Art, Kendall College of Art and Design, Grand Rapids, MI

Deborah Rockman, Chair of Drawing, Kendall College of Art and Design

Norwood Viviano, Assistant Professor of Art, Grand Valley State University

SUSTAINABILITY

Staff, Cascade Engineering, Grand Rapids, Michigan

2011

2D

Anne Ellegood, Senior Curator, Hammer Museum, Los Angeles

3D

Glenn Harper, Editor-in-Chief, *Sculpture Magazine*

TIME-BASED

Kathleen Forde, Artistic Director at Large, Borusan Contemporary, Istanbul

URBAN SPACE AND VENUE

Reed Kroloff, Director, Cranbrook Academy of Art and Art Museum

INTERNATIONAL

Nuit Banai, Art Historian and Critic, Tufts University, Boston

SUSTAINABILITY

Susan Lyons, Designer, New York

2012

JURIED GRAND PRIZE

Tom Eccles, Executive Director, Center for Curatorial Studies, Bard College

Theaster Gates, Artist, Director of Arts and Public Life, University of Chicago

Jerry Saltz, Senior Art Critic, *New York Magazine*

2D

Tyler Green, Art Journalist, Critic, *Modern Art Notes* and *Modern Painters*

3D

Lisa Freiman, Director of the Institute for Contemporary Art, Virginia Commonwealth University, Richmond, Virginia

TIME-BASED

Cathy Edwards, Director of Programming, International Festival of Arts and Ideas, New Haven, Connecticut

URBAN SPACE

Susan Szenasy, Editor-in-Chief, *Metropolis Magazine*

2013

JURIED GRAND PRIZE

Mel Chin, Artist

Anne Pasternak, President and Artistic Director, Creative Time, New York

Manon Slome, Co-founder and Chief Curator, No Longer Empty, New York

2D

John Yau, Poet, Critic, Professor of Critical Studies, Mason Gross School of the Arts, Rutgers University, New Brunswick, New Jersey

3D

Hesse McGraw, Vice President for Exhibitions and Public Programs, San Francisco Art Institute

TIME-BASED

Rashida Bumbray, Independent Curator, New York

URBAN SPACE

Eva Franch i Gilabert, Executive Director and Chief Curator, Storefront for Art and Architecture, New York

VENUE

Alice Gray Stites, Chief Curator and Director of Art Programming, 21c Museum Hotels, Louisville, Kentucky

ACKNOWLEDGMENTS

ArtPrize is a 501(c)(3) nonprofit organization that is made possible only through the generous support of organizations dedicated to sustaining the world's largest, radically open art competition:

FOUNDING SPONSOR:

The Dick & Betsy DeVos Family Foundation

THE DICK & BETSY DEVOS
FAMILY FOUNDATION

PREMIER LEADERSHIP SPONSORS INCLUDE:

Amway

The Richard and Helen DeVos Foundation

Founders Brewing Company

Kendall College of Art and Design of Ferris State University

Meijer

PNC Bank

The Rapid

LEADERSHIP SPONSORS INCLUDE:

Consumers Energy

The Daniel and Pamella DeVos Foundation

The Douglas and Maria DeVos Foundation

The Frey Foundation

Haworth

The Iserv Company

Steelcase Inc.

Subaru

Trivalent Group | HP

The VanderWeide Family Foundation

Wolverine Worldwide

Holland Litho made a generous in-kind printing donation.

ARTPRIZE

ArtPrize
How a Radically Open Competition
Transformed a City and Changed the
Way We Think about Art

Co-Project Director/Editor
Ben Mitchell, Duende Projects

Co-Project Director
Kevin Buist, Director of Exhibitions, ArtPrize

Editorial Review by Sigrid Asmus

Designed by Phil Kovacevich

Unless otherwise noted, all images by Brian Kelly Photography and Film, © ArtPrize.

Front cover: David Spriggs, *Vision*, 2010
Back cover: Mark Carpenter and Dan Johnson, *Lights in the Night*, 2012

ArtPrize
41 Sheldon Boulevard SE
Grand Rapids, Michigan 49504
www.artprize.org

Printed in the United States by Holland Litho

ISBN 978-0-615-96894-0